Where Are the

Sons and Daughters

of Ministry?

By

Michael D. Densmore

Where Are the Sons and Daughters of Ministry?

Author may be contacted at:
Bishop Michael D. Densmore Ministries
c/o Community Tabernacle
198 Selleck Street
Stamford, Connecticut 06902
(203) 961-1411
Email: bishopmd@optonline.net

Creative and printing services by:
CSN Books Publishing
"The Pastor's Publisher"
1975 Janich Ranch Road
El Cajon, CA 92019
Toll free: 866-484-6184

Table of Contents

Preface

This is the season where God is re-establishing apostolic government in the Kingdom. People are seeking for order within their ministries so they line up with the will of God for their lives. But as I travel, I continue to see the lack of accountability within the Body of Christ. Many times leaders have been hurt by poor or bad leadership, and have difficulty submitting to another leader. Yet, knowing that it is the Father's will to see us under apostolic government, many continue to wrestle with doing what is right due to their past experiences.

I believe, without a shadow of a doubt, that this is the time (like never before) to align yourself to the perfect will of God so you can see an end-time outpouring of God in your life.

Behold, I will send you Elijah the prophet before the coming of the great and dreadful day of the Lord:

And he shall turn the heart of the fathers to the children, and the heart of the children to their fathers, lest I come and smite the earth with a curse.

(Malachi 4:5-6)

I truly believe the Lord has turned the hearts of true apostolic fathers to the children, but there is a lack of children able to discern the times due to their unfavorable past experiences, so they are not seeking after the fathers. That is why fathers are asking the question: "Where are the sons and daughters of ministry? Where are the children of ministry in this last day move of God?"

This is the hour for prophetic fulfillment in the Kingdom; I believe we will see Kingdom manifestation unlike any time in our spiritual history. Yet, many in the five-fold ministry are hindering the full manifestation of God in the earthly realm because of being out of alignment.

I believe God will not allow anybody to hinder this great move. Since I believe the hearts of the fathers are turned toward the sons and daughters, let us take a spiritual journey in this book so the Holy Spirit can minister to us, and as a result, our hearts will be turned toward the apostolic fathers the Lord has placed in the Body.

As the children's hearts are turned toward the fathers, it will allow them to pour into us and pass on their apostolic mantles to the true sons and daughters so that we will be able to operate in another dimension of God for this last day move.

> *A bastard shall not enter into the congregation of the Lord; even to his tenth generation shall he not enter into the congregation of the Lord.*
>
> (Deuteronomy 23:2)

I pray this book ministers to you so you may find yourself in the posture of a son or daughter. As you do, you will avoid being positioned in the Body of Christ as a spiritual bastard, a fatherless child without apostolic authority and accountability in your life. Lack of accountability does not just affect you, it also impacts those you birth in the Body of Christ. Lack of yielding to authority will spiritually handicap sons and daughters in their ability to function in the congregation of the Lord.

There must be Kingdom order in this last hour!

I pray God will bless you to receive what He is saying in this hour so that you, and all who are spiritually connected to you, will enjoy the fullness of what the Lord has for your life and ministry in this hour.

Chapter One

Isaac, the Son of Abraham

The relationship of father and son was established from the beginning in the book of Genesis, the "book of beginnings." It is obvious that God intended parental order from the foundation of the Earth. From the beginning, Abraham, "the Father of Faith," had sons and daughters. God made a covenant with him in Genesis 12:2-3:

> *And I will make of thee a great nation, and I will bless thee, and make thy name great; and thou shalt be a blessing:*
>
> *And I will bless them that bless thee, and curse him that curseth thee: and in thee shall all families of the earth be blessed.*

This is the covenant the Lord made with Abraham as he walked in obedience to what the Lord commanded. I believe this covenant still applies to us as believers when we walk in obedience to what the Lord requires of His children. God did not just give Abraham a covenant, He also showed him a glimpse of what

He had in store for his life as he operated in faith and obedience to what the Lord commanded.

> *And the Lord said unto Abram, after that Lot was separated from him, lift up now thine eyes, and look from the place where thou art northward, and southward, and eastward, and westward:*
>
> *For all the land which thou seest, to thee will I give it, and to thy seed forever.*
>
> *And I will make thy seed as the dust of the earth: so that if a man can number the dust of the earth, then shall thy seed also be numbered.*
>
> *Arise, walk through the land in the length of it and in the breadth of it; for I will give it unto thee.*
>
> (Genesis 13: 14-17)

In all his lifetime, Abraham could never see the full manifestation of the Word of the Lord God had given to him. Therefore, he needed a seed that would continue the life of the promise and see its manifestation. Whenever God gives a promise to a father, I believe there will always be an heir to benefit from what God is going to do in the life of that spiritual father. But Abraham had a problem...he did not have a seed. I imagine he probably asked the Lord, "Where is my son?"

And I will bless her, and give thee a son also of her: yea, I will bless her, and she shall be a mother of nations; kings of people shall be of her.

And God said, Sarah thy wife shall bear thee a son indeed; and thou shalt call his name Isaac: and I will establish my covenant with him for an everlasting covenant and with his seed after him.
(Genesis 17: 16,19)

Abraham was one hundred years old and Sarah ninety years old when God gave His promise of a son to them!

Be careful not to move ahead of God when He has made you a promise. Be willing to wait on the son of promise, no matter how it looks, knowing that God is faithful to His promises.

For all the promises of God in him are yea, and in him amen, unto the glory of God by us.
(2 Corinthians 1: 20)

Learn to wait on the promises of God. You cannot make happen that which only God can bring to pass. Sarah did not wait on the manifestation of God, so she decided to assist God in manifesting His promise. Whenever you begin to try to assist God, you move from the promise to producing the son of the flesh.

Now Sarai, Abram's wife bare him no children: and she had a handmaid, an Egyptian, whose name was Hagar.

And Sarai said unto Abram, Behold now, the Lord hath restrained me from bearing: I pray thee, go in unto my maid; it may be that I may obtain children by her.

And Abram hearkened to the voice of Sarai. And the angel of the Lord said unto her, Behold thou art with child, and shalt bear a son, and shalt call his name Ishmael; because the Lord hath heard thy affliction.
(Genesis 16:1-2,11)

Apostolic fathers must be careful when seeking sons so that they do not produce sons of the flesh instead of sons of the promise. As the fathers are seeking God for the sons and daughters of ministry, let them be patient and wait on God's divine intervention. Whatever is produced in the flesh will not be able to carry out the God-given assignments in our lives.

I pray that as you read this book, God will minister to you. Regardless of how long you have been waiting on the son of the promise, continue to be faithful to what God has spoken to you. Know that He will do just what He said as you operate in faith.

And as for Ishmael, I have heard thee: Behold, I have blessed him, and will make him fruitful, and will multiply him exceedingly; twelve princes shall he beget and I will make him a great nation.

But my covenant will I establish with Isaac, which Sarah shall bear unto thee at this set time in the next year.
(Genesis 17:20-21)

Because the Lord is a covenant keeper, He imparts a blessing upon the son of the flesh, Ishmael. It is obvious that the sons who we seek after the flesh may experience blessings as a son, but the covenant is established with the son of promise, Isaac.

In addition, our sons and daughters of promise will carry out the promise God has given to us. If God's order is established via our God-given children, it is our responsibility to wait on the manifestation of our sons. If you have been wondering, "Where is the son?", just wait on the manifestation of God. As He spoke the promise, it shall come to pass.

> *And the Lord visited Sarah as he had said, and the Lord did unto Sarah as he had spoken.*
>
> *For Sarah conceived, and bare Abraham a son in his old age, at the set time of which God had spoken to him.*
> (Genesis 21:1-2)

As God kept His promise to Abraham, so shall He keep His promise to you as a son or daughter, to continue to the vision God has placed in your life.

Although Isaac was the son of promise, that relationship had to be tested. Let us take a close look at how God tested Abram (the father) and Isaac (the son) in their father and son relationship, the true test of sonship. When you identify with the children of your ministry, that relationship will be tested.

And it came to pass after these things, that God did tempt Abraham, and said unto him Abraham: and he said, Behold here I am.

And he said, Take now thy son, thine only son Isaac, whom thou lovest, and get thee into the land of Moriah; and offer him there for a burnt offering upon one of the mountains which I will tell thee of.

(Genesis 22: 1-2)

This is a dual test of fathership and sonship. The father must be willing to be obedient, dealing with the son or daughter's of promise, no matter how difficult it is. The father must trust the God of the promise in order to deal with the children of promise as God leads him. God is testing the father's love for Him as the God of the promise. We must love the God of the promise more than the son, which is part of the manifestation of the promise.

Do not start to love the manifestation of the promise so much that you neglect the God of the promise. Abraham was obedient with the test of the son of promise, establishing himself as a "Father of Faith." He trusted the God of promise to provide. He continued to look to God for the manifestation of the promise, and not to the son God had given to him.

> *And Abraham took the wood of the burnt offering, and laid it upon Isaac his son; and he took the fire in his hand, and a knife; and they went both of them together.*
>
> *And Isaac spake unto Abraham his father, and said, My father and he said, Here am I, my son. And he said , Behold the fire and the wood: but where is the lamb for a burnt offering?*
>
> *And Abraham said, My son, God will provide himself a lamb for a burnt offering; so they went both of them together.*
>
> (Genesis 22:6-8)

Notice the test of sonship here; the son is of age, but is still willing to lay down his life, to be a sacrifice for a burnt offering for his father. A true son will always trust his father with his life and ministry. The son recognized that his destiny rested in the hands of the father; he knew that his father would always do what is best for him, without killing his destiny. When the father was willing to offer the son as a sacrifice, and the son was willing to submit to spiritual authority, then they were both able to see God as Jehovah-Jireh, the Provider.

I have no doubt that this is the place God wants to bring the Body of Christ in this hour. Sons will have vision and provision as they position themselves under apostolic order as children of promise.

In your personal ministry, you will begin to see God as Jehovah-Jireh as you go to the mount of the Lord.

And Abraham called the name of that place Jehovah-jireh: as it is said to this day, in the mount of the Lord it shall be seen.
(Genesis 22:14)

Chapter Two

The Elijah and Elisha Relationship

I believe a true child will have the mantle, the ministry, and the anointing of the father. Many argue that the Elijah and Elisha relationship was more mentor than father, but I definitely believe that to be a child of an apostolic father, you do not need to be biologically birthed from his loins. There is a divine intervention; God strategically, divinely connects those together whom He has ordained to walk in apostolic order to bring forth a Kingdom manifestation in the earthly realm. This divine hook-up was manifested in the Elijah and Elisha relationship.

So he departed thence, and found Elisha the son of Shaphat, who was plowing with twelve yoke of oxen before him, and he with the twelfth: and Elijah passed by him, and cast his mantle upon him.

And he left the oxen and ran after Elijah, and said, Let me, I pray thee, kiss my father, and my mother, and then I will follow thee. And he said unto him, Go back again: for what have I done to thee?

And he returned back from him, and took a yoke of oxen, and slew them, and boiled their flesh with the instruments of the oxen, and gave unto the people, and they did eat. Then he arose, and went after Elijah, and ministered unto him.

(1 Kings 19:19-21)

Once Elijah's mantle was cast upon him, he ran after Elijah because he recognized God's divine intervention bringing him to the next dimension of God.

When the mantle of the father is upon the son, he will be willing to leave all and follow his apostolic father. The father will be able to recognize the son due to his willingness to forsake all else to follow.

When the mantle of the father is upon the son, the father will not have to wonder where his son is because the son will have an undying commitment to the father.

When the mantle of the father is upon the son, the father will have a level of sensitivity toward the son, allowing him to put some things in order so they will flow in apostolic order. Notice that Elijah allowed Elisha to go settle some things at home with his family and take care of personal affairs. Elijah understood that it would be difficult for Elisha to follow him with unresolved issues in his past, so he allowed him to resolve those issues. Then Elisha was able to follow Elijah, and more than follow, he ministered to him!

Sons do not just only follow, they minister to their fathers. Many fathers are asking, "Where are the sons and daughters of ministry?" because they find themselves always ministering to the children, but never receiving anything in return from the relationship.

The father and child relationship should be dual. The fathers minister to the children and the children minister to the fathers.

Frequently, other people and religious leaders do not understand the relationship that God has orchestrated. The ministry relationship will sometimes be challenged by those who believe they do not need that relationship to receive spiritual insight as to what God wants to do in their lives.

And the sons of the prophets that were at Bethel came forth to Elisha, and said unto him, Knowest thou that the Lord will take away thy master from thy head today? And he said, Yea, I know it, hold ye your peace.

And the sons of the prophets that were at Jericho came to Elisha, and said unto him, Knowest thou that the Lord will take away thy master from thy head today?   And he answered, Yea, I know it: hold ye your peace.

(2 Kings 2:3,5)

Notice that the sons of the prophets, the seers, only knew that Elijah was going to die, but they could not see how Elisha's destiny was tied to Elijah.   And so, on two occasions, we see the sons of the prophets trying to convince Elisha to stop following Elijah because he was going to die! When others cannot see your divine connection, you must be able to recognize it without a shadow of doubt because, if Elisha had been moved by the seers, he would have stopped following Elijah and missed his double portion!

When the mantle of an apostolic father has been cast on you, do not allow religious leaders to deter you from your divine relationship to experience the full manifestation of what God has for your ministry. It is clear that Elisha knew what he wanted, and he understood that Elijah had it.

> *And it came to pass, when they were gone over, that Elijah said unto Elisha, Ask what shall I do for thee, before I be taken away from thee. And Elisha said, I pray thee, let a double portion of thy spirit be upon me.*

> *And he said, Thou hast asked a hard thing: nevertheless, if thou see me when I am taken from thee, it shall be so unto thee: but if not, it shall not be so.*

> *And it came to pass, as they still went on, and talked, that, behold, there appeared a chariot of fire, and horses of fire, and parted them both asunder; and Elijah went up by a whirlwind into heaven.*

> *And Elisha saw it, and he cried, My father, my father, the chariot of Israel, and the horsemen thereof. And he saw him no more: and he took hold of his own clothes, and rent them in two pieces.*

> *He took up also the mantle of Elijah that fell from him and went back, and stood by the bank of Jordan.*

> (2 Kings 2: 9-13)

Elisha followed his personal conviction despite opposition, and he received the double portion God had for his ministry. I pray that you are seeing the spiritual paradigm that has gone before us. Elisha refers to Elijah as "father" as he is being taken up in the whirlwind. To receive from the father, you must *perceive* him as father, not just as a mentor for ministry and the perfecting of your God-given assignment.

> *And he took the mantle of Elijah that fell from him, and smote the waters, and said, Where is the Lord God of Elijah? And when he also had smitten the waters, they parted hither and thither: and Elisha went over.*
>
> *And when the sons of the prophets which were to view at Jericho saw him, they said, The spirit of Elijah doth rest on Elisha. And they came to meet him, and bowed themselves to the ground before him.*
>
> (2 Kings 2:14-15)

Here we see that his commitment to his father brings him into supernatural manifestations in his own ministry. He takes what he saw his father do, and repeats it in the same place his father had previously, getting the same results. This is only the beginning of the double portion in his life. Even those who had opposed

Elisha following Elijah witnessed the spirit of Elijah on his life and ministry, bowing on the ground before him.

If somebody is opposing your sonship to a specific apostolic father, do not be moved! Stay with your spiritual convictions and watch what God does in the life of your ministry. Those religious leaders, known as prophets, who had opposed Elisha following Elijah, ultimately bowed to the ground before him because they saw the spirit of his father upon his life.

The relationship of Elijah and Elisha is a great example to ministers who are struggling with submitting their lives to other men. It was through Elisha's submission that he was mentored and ministered to by the father, receiving the double portion for his ministry.

Friend, if you are in ministry, or even desire to be, I encourage you to prayerfully find your divine connection for the next dimension of your life and ministry. Position yourself as a son or daughter so the mantle of an apostolic father can be cast upon you. I totally believe that this is the will of God for our lives as sons and daughters.

It is time that our fathers stop walking around with a mantle, asking, "Where are the children?" We must not let our fathers take their mantles to the grave! Even though Elisha was fathered for ministry, I cannot find in the Scriptures where he passed on his mantle.

And Elisha died, and they buried him. And the bands of the Moabites invaded the land at the coming in of the year.

And it came to pass, as they were burying a man, that, behold, they spied a band of men; and they cast the man into the sepulchre of Elisha; and when the man was let down, and touched the bones of Elisha, he revived, and stood up on his feet.
(2 Kings 13:20-21)

Elisha was anointed to the very bones! The mantle on his life was so strong that a dead man was thrown into his grave and received his life back!

Some of you reading this book have ministries that seem to be dying. You need to grab the mantle of an apostolic father so that your ministry may live and not die. Be a son or daughter in ministry and watch God do some

Chapter Three

Timothy, the Son of Paul

Some reading this book may have noticed that I have used Old Testament patriarchs in the previous two chapters. I believe the Old Testament is our schoolmaster, and definitely a paradigm for New Testament order in the 21st century Church. But for those who may have difficulty with that paradigm, let us look at a New Testament apostle, Timothy, the spiritual son of the Apostle Paul.

Paul, an apostle of Jesus Christ by the commandment of God our Savior, and Lord Jesus Christ, which is our hope;

Unto Timothy, my own son in the faith: Grace, mercy and peace, from God our Father and Jesus Christ our Lord.
                                        (1 Timothy 1:1-2)

The salutation Paul uses to Timothy is "son," even though Paul was not his biological father. The relationship of the father and the children does not always need to be biological, but it *must* be spiritually connected by faith.

As you operate in the level of faith, it strengthens your divine connection, preparing you for the dimension of ministry in your life. Prayerfully ask yourself, "Is there an apostolic father in my life?" Do you have someone you refer to as your son or daughter in ministry? If not, why? You need a spiritual father for your life, and you need to be a spiritual father to a son or daughter in ministry.

Know that there is an apostolic father in the Body Christ that God has orchestrated just for your life and ministry. That apostolic father could be right now asking God, "Where is my son or daughter in ministry?" Have you positioned yourself to be fathered, or sought the Lord for your apostolic father? Could it be you feel there is no need for an apostolic father? Or, is it because of your past, hurtful experiences in the Body of Christ? In the natural, every son or daughter has a father; as it is in the natural, so shall it be in the spirit!

I have heard many leaders declare, "The Lord is my apostolic father." That is like saying that sheep do not need a shepherd! I know none of these men would agree with a Christian in their congregation who said, "I do not need a pastor because the Lord is my shepherd." Trust the people God has placed in the Body to impart into our lives and equip us for Kingdom business in the earthly realm.

Pray and seek out a spiritual father. Submit your gifts to them because that is the apostolic order. If our congregation does not see us submitting to spiritual authority, it could cause chaos in our ministry. People tend to emulate those they serve under; lack of accountability in leadership could cause them to diminish your own spiritual authority in their lives.

> *And there shall be, like people, like priest: and I will punish them for their ways, and reward them their doings.*
> (Hosea 4:9)

The spiritual father has spiritual authority over your life, and also prays for you regarding the things of God and the everyday cares of life's issues that you face in ministry.

> *I thank God, whom I serve from my forefathers with pure conscience, that without ceasing I have remembrance of thee in my prayers night and day.*
> (2 Timothy 1:3)

The spiritual father encourages you and stirs up the gifts of God in your life. Notice, Paul never discredited those who imparted into his life as fathers, but celebrated what they had done for him. Obviously, what they had imparted into his life had given him the humility to submit to an apostolic father without a struggle.

Allow your spiritual father the opportunity to stir up and push you to the next level of ministry.

Paul affirms the ministry and call of God in Timothy's life through the laying on of hands.

> *When I call to remembrance the unfeigned faith that is in thee, which dwelt first in thy grandmother Lois, and thy mother Eunice; and I am persuaded that in thee also.*
>
> *Wherefore I put thee in remembrance that thou stir up the gift of God, which is in thee by the putting on of my hands.*
>
> (2 Timothy 1:5-6)

We need to be affirmed by an apostolic father publicly. This affirmation demonstrates to the local church community where we serve that an apostolic father acknowledges that we have been tested, tried and found worthy to be operating in the capacity of ministry which we have been called.

Many people operating in ministry cannot trace their legitimacy. If there is a problem in the local church or community, who do you turn to for disciplinary actions (if necessary) when the leader is not under spiritual accountability? Everything that God established has order, a check and balance system. But many in the five-fold ministries operate outside of these biblical parameters.

Many are threatened by accountability; they totally rebel against it, establishing denominations or reformations that satisfy their own personal parameters. That is why apostolic fathers are still asking the question, "Where are the sons and daughters of ministry who desire spiritual accountability and spiritual authority?"

The father also pours into the sons and daughters based on his past experiences. This input helps them to avoid some of the pitfalls of ministry. We constantly see Paul encouraging, warning, exhorting and establishing doctrinal teaching to Timothy.

If you are in the five-fold ministry, and minister to the flock of God, ask yourself: "Who pours warnings and exhortations into our life?" This is one of the more important roles of the apostolic father to the sons and daughters of ministry.

> *Thou therefore, my son, be strong in the grace that is in Christ Jesus.*
>
> *And the things that thou hast heard of me among many witnesses, the same commit thou to faithful men, who shall be able to teach others also.*
>
> *Thou therefore endure hardness as a good soldier of Jesus Christ.*
> (2 Timothy 2:1-3)
>
> *But watch thou in all things, endure afflictions, do the work of an evangelist, make full proof of thy ministry.*
> (2 Timothy 4:5)

All of us, sometimes in our lives, need encouragement due to the challenging situations we frequently encounter in ministry. Thanks be to God for apostolic fathers who have gone before us, and can now give us strength and wise counsel!

Where no counsel is, the people fall: but in the multitude of counselors there is safety.

(Proverbs 11:14)

Our counselors help keep our ministries on course, avoiding possible shipwrecks. Our apostolic fathers help us stay in the safe lane, warning us of potential problems, and helping us to avoid fatal accidents in our ministries. As anyone reading this book knows, when a ministry collapses, it does not just impact the leader, many other lives can be destroyed.

We have looked at some Old Testament patriarchs: Isaac, son to Abraham; and Elisha, son to Elijah. We have seen in the New Testament that Timothy was a son to Paul. But now, let us look at the perfect example in the Scriptures...Jesus, as the Son of God.

Chapter Four

Jesus, the Son of God

Jesus, being divine in nature, took on a natural body to be an example to us, to show us the importance of sonship in the earthly realm. Being God in the heavens, He still could have done everything necessary for us in the Spirit (without taking on the only begotten Son of the Father). But Jesus found it important to us as a people to see a visual example of true sonship. The Scriptures prior to His coming were clear; He would establish a King pattern to bring forth a Kingdom manifestation in the earthly realm.

Now the birth of Jesus Christ was on this wise: when as his mother Mary was espoused to Joseph, before they came together, she was found with child of the Holy Ghost.

Then Joseph her husband, being a just man, and not willing to make her a public example, was minded to put her away privily.

But while he thought on these things, behold the angel of the Lord appeared unto him in a dream, saying, Joseph, thou son of David, fear not to take unto thee Mary thy wife; for that which is conceived in her is of the Holy Ghost.

And she shall bring forth a son and thou shalt call his name Jesus: for he shall save his people from their sins.
(Matthew 1:18-21)

It is definitely clear that Jesus was conceived of the Holy Ghost and came via natural means through the virgin Mary. The Father, being God, trusted a natural man, Joseph, to serve as His earthly father. If God trusted an earthly being to serve as His only begotten Son's father, then what makes us think that He has suddenly changed the pattern?

Clearly, the example of Jesus refutes those in the Body of Christ who continue to insist, "I do not need a spiritual father. God is my father!" Leader, recognize God's pattern! He has entrusted an earthly father for your life and ministry!

Jesus had a normal young life as a child, with accountability to His earthly parents.

*And the child grew, and waxed strong in
spirit, filled with wisdom: and the grace of
God was upon him.*

(Luke 2:40)

As He submitted to His earthly father, we
begin to see the manifestation of His heavenly
Father upon His life. I believe the same is true
for us.   As we submit to earthly spiritual
authority, we will begin to see the perfect will of
God performed in our lives as sons and daughters
in ministry.

*And when they found him not, they turned
back again to Jerusalem, seeking him.*

*And it came to pass, that after three days
they found him in the temple, sitting in the
midst of the doctors, both hearing them,
and asking them questions.*

*And all that heard him were astonished at
his understanding and answers.*

*And when they saw him, they were amazed;
and his mother said unto him, Son why
hast thou thus dealt with us? Behold, thy
father and I have sought thee sorrowing.*

*And he said unto them, How is it that ye
sought me? Wist ye not that I must be about
my father's business?*

(Luke 2:45-49)

Through these Scriptures, we see the shift
from the son of Joseph to the Son of God. Jesus
had fulfilled His time with Joseph as father, and
now He is ready to pursue and fulfill His destiny
as the Son of God. However, note that Joseph
continued as His earthly father while Jesus went
about fulfilling the mission of His heavenly
Father.

Jesus continued to be a son throughout
Scripture; He obeyed that which the Father had
assigned to His hand. So too, as you fulfill your
God-given purpose, you must submit to a
spiritual father. Does someone currently call you
their son or daughter? Or, are they asking the
question, "Where are the sons and daughters of
ministry?"

Let us continue this journey with Jesus as
the Son of God as He follows the pattern that had
been laid down in the New Testament for
baptism.

*Then cometh Jesus from Galilee to Jordan
unto John, to be baptized of him.*

38

But John forbade him, saying, I have need to be baptized of thee, and comest thou to me?

And Jesus answering said unto him, Suffer it to be so now: for thus it becometh us to fulfill all righteousness. Then he suffered him.

And Jesus, when he was baptized, went up straightway out of the water: and lo, the heavens were opened unto him, and he saw the Spirit of God descending like a dove, and lighting upon him:

And lo a voice from heaven, saying, This is my beloved Son in whom I am well pleased.
(Matthew 3:13-17)

We hear God the Father affirming His Son: "This is my beloved Son in whom I am well pleased." Affirmation by an apostolic father is definitely the will of God; it was so important that God publicly affirmed His only begotten Son.

I pray that this book is ministering to your Spirit on the importance of being a son or daughter in ministry. Again, I ask the question, "Who has affirmed you, and who can refer to you as son or daughter?" Is your divine apostolic connection somewhere asking, "Where is my son or daughter?"

After this affirmation by the Father, Jesus began to operate in the full magnitude of His ministry.

Here is a question for consideration and prayer: Could it be that your ministry is being hindered because there is no one you have trusted to affirm and release you in the apostolic flow of God?

Jesus was able to operate in the full magnitude of His ministry, *and* was able to conquer His temptation.

> *Then saith Jesus unto him, Get thee hence, Satan: for it is written, Thou shalt worship the Lord thy God, and him only shalt thou serve.*
>
> *Then the devil leaveth him, and behold, angels came and ministered unto him.*
> (Matthew 4:10-11)

I believe many of the pitfalls of ministry could be avoided if we yielded ourselves to spiritual authority. Apostolic fathers play an important role in our lives to prepare and warn us of our own personal failures in life. Passing the temptation test, Jesus was able to continue the ministry throughout the gospels, operating in the anointing of His heavenly Father.

> *The Spirit of the Lord is upon me, because he hath anointed me, to preach the gospel to the poor, he hath sent me to heal the brokenhearted, to preach deliverance to the captives, and recovering of sight to the blind, to set at liberty them that are bruised,*
>
> *To preach the acceptable year of the Lord.*
> (Luke 4:18-19)

Jesus did that which He was anointed to do throughout the Scriptures; He completed His task so well that He was able to declare that the Scripture had been fulfilled.

> *And he began to say unto them, This day is this scripture fulfilled in your ears.*
> (Luke 4:21)

Jesus submitted to the Father; He understood the Father/Son relationship because, before He started His ministry, He chose twelve men to walk with Him in ministry. In reality, Jesus did not need to have people in His life to fulfill His destiny. However, He knew He would not be able to fulfill all that God had placed in Him, so He imparted His ministry to these men so that the life of the ministry would continue after His death and resurrection through the life of His sons.

> *And he goeth up into a mountain, and calleth unto him whom he would: and they came unto him.*
>
> *And he ordained twelve, that they should be with him, and that he might send them forth to preach.*
>
> *And to have power to heal sickness, and to cast out devils.*
>
> (Mark 3:13-15)

These men would continue the work of their spiritual Father after His death, burial and resurrection because of what He had imparted in there lives to equip them for the ministry after His departure from Earth to heaven. They were very concerned when they knew He was leaving, and that is why they wanted to see the Father one more time.

Thomas saith unto him, Lord, we know not whither thou goest; and how can we know the way?

Jesus saith unto him, I am the way, the truth, and the life: no man cometh unto the father but by me.

If ye had known me, ye should have known my father also: and from henceforth ye know him, and have seen him.

Philip saith unto him, Lord, shew us the father, and it sufficeth us.

Jesus saith unto him, Have I been so long time with you, and yet hast thou not known me, Philip? he that hath seen me hath seen the Father; and how sayest thou the, Shew us the Father?

(John 14:5-9)

Jesus let them know that when they saw Him they saw the Father because they are one. He had come to fulfill, in the earthly realm, a heavenly mandate for His life on Earth. Jesus was able to declare that when they saw Him, they saw the Father; He was carrying the mandate of His heavenly Father as the only begotten Son.

As a son or a daughter, you have a vision in life; what God has called you to do will be manifested in your ministry. As Jesus carried out the assignment of His Father, He was given a name above every other name, because of His submission to the will of His Father.

> *That at the name of Jesus every knee should bow, of things in heaven and things in earth, and things under earth;*
>
> *And that every tongue should confess that Jesus Christ is Lord to the glory of God the Farther.*
>
> (Philippians 2:10-11)

As Jesus, the Son of God, surrendered and submitted to the Father, His Name became great.

Could your greatness be hindered because you do not have an apostolic father in your life? Do you lack submission to a spiritual authority?

When you begin to be the provision for another person's vision, your vision becomes manifested. So, I encourage you to position yourself as a son or a daughter in ministry. That is God's Kingdom order. Then you will see the full manifestation of what God has spoken to or showed you.

I pray that soon the fathers will not be asking, "Where are the sons and daughters in ministry?"

I pray that all church leaders will submit to an apostolic relationship so we can soon see the prophetic fulfillment in the Body of Christ.